Mass-Marketing Fraud: A Threat Assessment

International Mass-Marketing Fraud Working Group

June 2010

TABLE OF CONTENTS

EXECUTIVE SUMMARY

The Nature, Scope, and Impact of Mass-Marketing Fraud

- Mass-marketing fraud has gradually transformed from a predominantly North American crime problem into a pervasive global criminal threat. (P. 4)

- There are strong indications that the order of magnitude of global mass-marketing fraud losses is in the tens of billions of dollars per year. (P. 5)

- For some victims, the risks extend well beyond loss of personal savings or funds to include physical threats or risks, loss of their homes, depression, and even contemplated, attempted, or actual suicide. (P. 7)

- Mass-marketing fraud has a substantial impact on economies and markets by undermining consumer trust and confidence in legitimate businesses. (P. 9)

- Large-scale criminal mass-marketing fraud operations are present in multiple countries in most regions of the world. (P. 9) Similarities between such operations include targeting victims in other countries, foreign outsourcing of operations, and involvement of organized criminal enterprises. (Pp. 10-13)

Methods and Techniques of Mass-Marketing Fraud

- As a whole, fraudulent mass-marketing operations are increasingly transnational, interconnected, and fluid, with groups shifting alliances according to the particular needs of a scheme. (P. 14)

- Fraudulent mass-marketers reach victims via all modes of communication – postal service, telephone, e-mail, Internet sites, television, radio, and even in person. (P. 16)

- Viable mass-marketing fraud groups require a variety of resources to operate, including the means to target and communicate with prospective victims, obtain and launder illicit proceeds, and evade law enforcement detection and investigation. These include legitimate business services, lead lists, communications tools, payment processors, fraudulent identification documents, and counterfeit financial instruments. (P. 17)

- Mass-marketing fraud criminals continue to use counterfeit financial instruments, including checks and money orders, to facilitate many mass-marketing schemes, including overpayment, lottery, and employment fraud. (P. 18)

- Operators of mass-marketing fraud schemes are highly adaptive, rapidly changing their methods and techniques to reduce the risks of law enforcement detection and investigation and to respond to consumer and business awareness of their current methods. (P. 19)

- Identity theft and money laundering continue to be critical components of various mass-marketing fraud schemes. (P. 20) One disturbing trend is the increasing exploitation of fraud victims to receive and launder victim funds, or to receive and disburse counterfeit financial instruments. (P. 22)

- While most mass-marketing fraud schemes are nonviolent in nature, law enforcement intelligence reveals that some fraud groups employ threats and coercive tactics against uncooperative victims, rival groups, and their own group members. (P. 23) Recent law enforcement intelligence suggests that use of mass-marketing related intra- and inter-group violence is on the rise in some places, such as Jamaica, Nigeria, and the United States. (P. 23)

Conclusion

- To counter the threat of mass-marketing fraud effectively, investigative, law enforcement, and regulatory authorities in multiple countries – whether those countries are used as bases of operations for mass-marketing fraud schemes, targets of such schemes, or both -- will need to pursue five approaches in close coordination. Those include (1) expansion of their capability to gather and share intelligence on all aspects of mass-marketing fraud schemes and their key participants; (2) development and expansion of capacities for disruption of the operations of mass-marketing fraud schemes through lawful means (e.g., seizure of counterfeit financial instruments and documents used in such schemes); (3) expansion of public awareness and education programs to help individuals and businesses more readily recognize solicitations by mass-marketing fraud schemes and take action to avoid or minimize losses to such schemes; (4) development of effective measures to more promptly identify and support victims of mass-marketing fraud schemes through public- and private-sector resources; and (5) development and expansion of coordinated efforts among investigative, law enforcement, and regulatory agencies to use their enforcement powers against major mass-marketing fraud schemes. (Pp. 24-25)

INTRODUCTION

Mass-marketing fraud is a term increasingly used around the world to refer to fraud schemes that use mass-communications media – including telephones, the Internet, mass mailings, television, radio, and even personal contact – to contact, solicit, and obtain money, funds, or other items of value from multiple victims in one or more jurisdictions. Although law enforcement and regulatory authorities often use a variety of names to refer to the phenomenon – including "advance-fee fraud," "419 fraud," "Internet fraud," and "telemarketing fraud" – the growing profusion of labels for these fraud schemes tends to obscure the fact that such schemes often are conducted using multiple communications channels to identify and contact victims, as well as identical or highly similar methods of operation that are not dependent on a single communications medium.

Today, mass-marketing fraud schemes operate from, and increasingly seek to target victims in, numerous countries on multiple continents. Moreover, such schemes are aware and take advantage of differences between countries in legislative authorities prohibiting such schemes. As a consequence, mass-marketing fraud has become a substantial concern for law enforcement in several regions of the world.

The International Mass-Marketing Fraud Working Group (IMMFWG) prepared this threat assessment to provide governments and the public with a current assessment of the nature and scope of the threat that mass-marketing fraud poses around the world. The IMMFWG, which was established in September 2007, consists of law enforcement, regulatory, and consumer protection agencies from seven countries, including Australia, Belgium, Canada, the Netherlands, Nigeria, the United Kingdom, and the United States, as well as Europol. The IMMFWG seeks to facilitate the multinational exchange of information and intelligence, the coordination of cross-border operations to detect, disrupt, and apprehend mass-marketing fraud, and the enhancement of public-awareness and public-education measures concerning international mass-marketing fraud schemes.

The information and analysis in this assessment is current through May 2010, and are derived principally from public and non-public law enforcement and non-law enforcement sources in Australia, Belgium, Canada, the Netherlands, Nigeria, the United Kingdom, and the United States.

I.   THE NATURE, SCOPE, AND IMPACT OF MASS-MARKETING FRAUD

Over the last two decades, according to law enforcement authorities in multiple countries, mass-marketing fraud has gradually transformed from a predominantly North American crime problem into a pervasive global criminal threat. This section of the Threat Assessment discusses the current scope and scale of mass-marketing fraud as a crime problem. The available evidence indicates that mass-marketing fraud schemes generate losses estimated at tens of billions of dollars each year from millions of individuals and businesses around the world. These schemes typically benefit members of criminal organizations and groups, while devastating the lives and financial well-being of victims and their families.

The Nature of Mass-Marketing Fraud

Mass-marketing fraud – whether committed via the Internet, telemarketing "boiler rooms," the mail, television or radio advertising, mass meetings, or even one-on-one talks over people's kitchen tables[1] -- has two elements in common. First, the criminals who conduct any mass-marketing fraud scheme aim to defraud multiple individuals or businesses to maximize their criminal revenues. Second, the schemes invariably depend on persuading victims to transfer money or funds to the criminals based on promises of valuable goods, services, or benefits, then never delivering the promised goods, services, or benefits to the victims.

Today, law enforcement officials see a broader array of mass-marketing fraud schemes than ever before, using a variety of "pitches" (explanations of promised goods, services, or benefits) such as lottery or sweepstakes winnings, investment or business opportunities, schemes that involve use of counterfeit checks, and "romance" schemes in which victims are made to believe that the persons contacting them have sincere romantic feelings for them. (A more extensive list of mass-marketing fraud schemes can be found in the Appendix.)

Mass-Marketing Fraud Losses

At present, there are no comprehensive and authoritative statistical data regarding the scope of mass-marketing fraud on a global level. A number of countries – notably, Belgium, Canada, the Netherlands, the United Kingdom, and the United States -- currently operate or are developing national mass-marketing fraud and/or Internet fraud reporting centers. Even so, many mass-marketing fraud victims who try to report their losses typically direct their complaints to countless private sector companies and local, state, provincial, national, and international law enforcement agencies. This substantially hinders efforts to track fraud losses and determine victimization rates.[2]

Furthermore, many victims who lose money to mass-marketing fraud do not contact authorities or reporting centers. Their reasons range from shame, embarrassment, and perceptions of law enforcement inaction to fear of being prosecuted for participating in schemes to embezzle funds from companies and countries. Elderly victims, in particular, often may be unable or unwilling to report due to diminished mental faculties or fear of losing financial independence should their families discover the fraud. While it is impossible to know how many victims fail to report fraud, the number is likely substantial. Belgium has estimated that unreported mass-marketing fraud incidents likely exceed the official national average of 66 percent for all crimes. A 2007 Canadian consumer fraud survey found that almost nine in ten victims do not report fraudulent solicitations.[3] The United Kingdom's Office of Fair Trading offers a starker estimate, suggesting that fewer than five percent of people report fraudulent solicitations to appropriate authorities.[4]

Nonetheless, from analysis of consumer fraud surveys and other data, including fraud complaint data and extrapolations from data in various schemes uncovered by law enforcement, there are strong indications that the order of magnitude of global mass-marketing fraud losses is in the tens of billions of dollars per year:

There are strong indications that the order of magnitude of global mass-marketing fraud losses is in the tens of billions of dollars per year.

- ***Fraud Surveys***. A 2006 United Kingdom Office of Fair Trading (OFT) study estimated that each year 3.2 million United Kingdom adults (6.5 percent of the adult population) fall victim to mass-marketing schemes, collectively losing £3.5 billion.[5] Similarly, a June 2008 study by the Australian Bureau of Statistics (ABS) found that in 2007, 806,000 Australians aged 15 years and over (5 percent of the population) were victims of at least one incident of personal fraud in the preceding 12 months, including selected schemes such as lottery, pyramid, and phishing schemes, and that 453,100 of those victims (56.2 percent) reportedly lost AU $977 million (US $905.7 million as of June 27, 2008).[6]

  While there is no comparable survey of adult U.S. fraud victims limited to mass-marketing fraud, a 2005 survey by the United States Federal Trade Commission (FTC) estimated that 30.2 million consumers (13.5 percent of U.S. adults) may have been victims of various consumer fraud schemes (including foreign lottery and prize-promotion schemes) during the preceding year.[7] Extrapolations from the percentages of Australian and United Kingdom adults victimized by fraud and their reported losses would indicate that an equivalent percentage of U.S. adults would lose approximately $23 to $25 billion a year to mass-marketing fraud.[8] While Belgium has not conducted a recent fraud survey, Belgian police have analyzed cases in a national police database and extrapolated, based on estimated failure-to-report rates, that Belgian victims of Internet fraud may have lost more than €10 million in 2008.

- ***Complaint Data***. In a February 2010 report of complaints that it received in 2009 through its Consumer Sentinel network, stated that a total of 630,604 complaints reported total consumer fraud losses of more than $1.7 billion (i.e., $1,715,973,109), with an average loss of $2,721. Although the total consumer fraud loss reported to the FTC in 2008 was slightly higher at more than $1.8 billion (i.e., $1,835,032,926), the number of victims reporting losses was significantly smaller than the number in

2009 (i.e., 539,657 in 2008 versus 630,604 in 2009).[9] One indication that these data reflect losses from mass-marketing fraud schemes is the remarkable statement that in 2009, 117 consumers reported to the FTC that they had paid $1 million or more in fraud losses.[10]

> *In 2009, 117 U.S. consumers reported that they each had lost $1 million or more to fraud.*

As points of comparison, the Canadian Anti-Fraud Centre received more than 40,000 complaints and documented reported fraud losses of nearly CA $ 59.3 million in 2009,[11] and the Australian Competition and Consumer Commission received more than 20,000 scam-related complaints and inquiries in 2009, with aggregate reported losses of AU $69.9 million.[12]

Law enforcement and regulatory authorities acknowledge that the actual numbers of mass-marketing fraud victims and losses vastly exceed those reported to law enforcement and consumer protection agencies. In addition to the 2005 FTC survey mentioned above, a 2007 study commissioned by the Competition Bureau of Canada concluded that nearly 60 percent of the population, or approximately 15 million adult Canadians, had been the target of a mass-marketing scheme in the prior 12 months.[13]

- *Law Enforcement Actions*. Various law enforcement actions around the world have found mass-marketing fraud operations that each generate hundreds of millions of dollars or more in fraud losses. These include:

  - *Money-Transfer Schemes*. In July 2009, in a series of coordinated raids, Thai law enforcement authorities arrested 94 individuals, operating out of 11 rented homes in Chiang Mai, who conducted an international money-transfer scheme that was estimated to have taken in more than $710 million.[14]

  - *Ponzi and Investment Schemes*. Numerous Ponzi schemes (schemes in which fraudsters use funds paid by later victims to pay a portion of funds to earlier victims) and pyramid schemes in addition to the Bernard Madoff scheme have reportedly taken in billions of dollars in investor funds. One study by the Associated Press reported finding more than 150 Ponzi schemes that collapsed in 2009 alone, resulting in $16.5 billion in losses.[15] In April 2010, for example, a U.S. federal judge sentenced a Minnesota businessman to 50 years imprisonment for conducting a $3.7 billion Ponzi scheme whose victims included hedge funds, pastors, and retirees.[16] Other U.S. defendants recently have pleaded guilty to charges stemming from operation of Ponzi schemes that ranged as high as $1.2 billion.[17] In an entirely separate case, an Australian businessman was sought for arrest in connection with his alleged conduct of a Ponzi scheme that took in more than US $1.2 billion.[18]

One factor that appears likely to keep victim losses higher is the practice of many mass-marketing fraud schemes to target their victims for revictimization, either through further requests for funds in the same scheme or through later solicitations in which the fraudsters falsely claim that they are affiliated with law enforcement or the legal system and can help victims obtain the funds they previously lost. The 2006 OFT study concluded that mass-marketing fraud victims have a 30 percent chance of falling victim to a second fraudulent solicitation within 12 months of the initial incident, likely because their names are included on fraudsters' lists of individuals susceptible to deceptive solicitations. A 2003 survey by the AARP (formerly known as the American Association of Retired Persons) found that the risk of revictimization varies by fraud type: half of the lottery fraud victims and 27 percent of the investment fraud victims interviewed for the survey indicated they had experienced at least one additional instance of fraud within the prior three years.[19]

**Arrests of Alleged Participants in Chiang Mai Money-Transfer Scheme
[Source: Chiang Mai Mail]**

Financial losses, however, do not fully reflect all of the costs that mass-marketing fraud victims often bear. For some victims, the risks extend well beyond loss of personal savings or funds to include physical risks, loss of their homes, depression, and even contemplated, attempted, or actual suicide:

- **Physical Risks**. Although it is not widely recognized, some mass-marketing fraud victims find themselves subject to physical threats or risks stemming directly from their contact with the schemes. In recent years, law enforcement agencies have even documented several incidents in which mass-marketing fraud victims were induced to travel to various African countries, then kidnapped and held for ransom.[20] In 2008, for example, a Japanese businessman who believed that he was placing money into an investment opportunity traveled to South Africa, where he was kidnapped and held for $5 million ransom. Ultimately, one South African national and six Nigerian nationals were arrested for the kidnapping.[21]

  In addition, in some cases after the victim has admitted to a family member how much money they have lost, the victim may also become a victim of physical abuse:

> A 52 year old woman in the United States lost more than $44,000 to an inheritance scheme operated out of the Netherlands. As a result of losing the $44,000, she was physically abused by her husband and eventually fled the home.

- **Loss of Home.** Law enforcement and regulatory investigations have periodically found cases in which mass-marketing fraud victims either mortgage their homes to make payments to the fraud scheme or are forced to sell their homes to satisfy outstanding debts. Here are two examples, drawn from recent mass-marketing fraud investigations:

  > A 67 year old man in the United States lost more than $570,000 to an inheritance scam. The man, who was college-educated and owned his own company, sent money to Belgium, Germany, the Ivory Coast, the Netherlands, Spain, and the United Kingdom. In particular, he traveled to Amsterdam, where he was shown a trunk of money, was given a few bills which were good, and became convinced the funds were real. As a result of his losses, the man lost his life savings, his business, and his home, filed for bankruptcy, had to return to his native country to live with his relatives, and is being treated for depression.

  > A 76 year old man in the United States lost $87,000 of his personal funds to an inheritance scheme. After depleting his savings account to pay the required advance "fees," the man received "loans" in the form of counterfeit checks mailed from Canada to pay for additional nonexistent "fees." The face amounts of the counterfeit checks totaled $482,466. After he deposited the checks and remitted funds back to the fraudsters, his bank placed liens on his bank accounts and his residence. In the course of the scheme he sent money to Canada, Japan, the Netherlands, and the United Kingdom. Ultimately the man lost his residence to foreclosure and he is now living on Social Security payments.

- **Depression**. When mass-marketing fraud schemes cause substantial losses to victims, victims often have reported that they find the losses emotionally devastating. The stress and pain of victimization may manifest themselves as depression, withdrawal and isolation from family and friends, difficulty at work, and the deterioration of physical and mental health.

- **Contemplated, Attempted, or Actual Suicide**. For some time, law enforcement investigators have handled mass-marketing fraud cases in which at least one victim who had suffered devastating financial losses had committed or admitted having considered suicide. Although there is no systematic means of gathering such information from previous cases, an ongoing survey by the Working Group has been able to document at least 27 cases of mass-marketing fraud victims in various countries who had considered, attempted, or committed suicide since January 1, 2006 as a result of their fraud losses. Here are a few examples of those cases:

> A 56-year-old woman who lived in the United States committed suicide in 2006 after becoming a victim of a lottery fraud scheme and sending the scheme more than $400,000. The woman, a college graduate, reportedly responded to an email solicitation, then sent various wire transfers to individuals located in Amsterdam.

> A husband and wife, both 65 years old, who live in the United Kingdom have together lost more than $2.7 million dollars to an inheritance scam being operated out of China, the Netherlands, and Spain. The couple used their life savings, re-financed their home, and withdrew retirement funds to pay for the advance fees that the scheme charged. As a result of the losses, the wife has attempted suicide twice. Currently the couple is in the process of losing their home to foreclosure and is being treated for depression.

> A retirement-age man who lives in Australia lost more than $6.1 million to an investment scheme. The man, who had been a successful businessman before the fraud, eventually admitted to authorities that he could no longer walk to the bus stop in his neighborhood because each time he did so he felt a temptation to step in front of an oncoming bus.

Finally, mass-marketing fraud has a substantial impact on economies and markets by undermining consumer trust and confidence in legitimate businesses. The Office of Fair Trading reports that "more than half of [United Kingdom] scam victims admitted to having changed their purchasing and payment behavior, generally becoming more cautious or suspicious of any contact that could potentially be another scam."[22] In contrast, less than a quarter of respondents who had been targeted but not defrauded by fraudulent solicitations claimed to have changed their behavior. Approximately 15 percent of all respondents indicated that they had reduced their online shopping. A small number of victims also claimed that they were more likely to limit their use of credit cards, dispose of unsolicited mail, and ignore cold callers and unsolicited offers.

The Global Scope of Mass-Marketing Fraud

Over time, mass-marketing fraud has developed into a global crime problem. Today, large-scale criminal mass-marketing fraud operations are present in multiple countries in most regions of the world. Recent law enforcement investigations have exposed such schemes operating not only in multiple countries in North America, Europe, and Africa, but in other countries and jurisdictions as diverse as Brazil, Costa Rica, Hong Kong, India, Israel, the Philippines, Thailand, and the United Arab Emirates.

Large-scale criminal mass-marketing fraud operations are present in multiple countries in most regions of the world.

Analysis of the fraud operations in these countries increasingly reveals more similarities than differences. Some of the most important similarities are as follows.

- *Targeting of Victims in Other Countries*. Intelligence suggests that numerous mass-marketing fraud operations on multiple continents attempt to evade detection and identification by targeting victims in other countries.[23]

  > *Africa.* Although the global proliferation of autonomous West African fraud groups has altered, to varying degrees, Nigeria's role as an epicenter of fraudulent operations, a home to criminal kingpins, and a destination for illicit proceeds, Nigeria continues to serve as a base of operations for a wide range of mass-marketing activity. Recent law enforcement intelligence indicates that Nigeria-based fraudsters conduct international advance-fee schemes, black money schemes targeting Middle Eastern victims, and the fraudulent purchase of merchandise via the Internet. In addition to overseas victims, Nigeria-based mass-marketers increasingly target middle- and upper-class citizens of Nigeria and nearby African countries.

  > At the same time, mass-marketing fraud has expanded into numerous quarters of sub-Saharan Africa. In recent years, law enforcement investigations have uncovered new mass-marketing fraud operations in Benin, Cote D'Ivoire, Ghana, South Africa, Togo, and Uganda, from which locations perpetrators are conducting 419 schemes and producing counterfeit checks. Law enforcement investigations have determined that large numbers of local Ghanaian youngsters participate in fraud schemes that target foreign victims. In January 2009 Ghanaian authorities estimated that the Ghana Post was seizing and destroying as many as 1,000 mass-marketing fraud letters each day, the majority destined for individuals in the United Kingdom and the United States. In addition, in March 2010 Chinese media reported the arrest of nine Cameroonians who had obtained nearly $40,000 from a Fujian province resident who had been contacted by fraudsters through a dating website.[24]

  > *Asia*: In November 2009, Thai police arrested four Chinese nationals based in Bangkok who used both telemarketing and the Internet to defraud Chinese and Taiwanese residents out of nearly $1 million. The fraudsters reportedly called their intended victims, pretending to be Taiwanese Interpol authorities and prosecutors, and told them told their bank accounts could be seized by authorities after they were caught up in a fraud scheme. Victims were told that to avoid having their money seized, they should transfer their money to bank accounts in Thailand. The scheme also reportedly faxed to victims copies of a fake arrest warrant issued by a Taipei court in order to intimidate them.[25]

  > *Australia/New Zealand*: Both Australia and New Zealand are targeted by mass-marketing fraud schemes operating from Europe and Africa for online lottery, car-sales, and counterfeit-check fraud schemes.[26] The Queensland Police Service recently reported that residents of that state were sending between AU $800,000 and $1 million per month to fraud schemes in Nigeria.[27] Both countries also are home to fraudulent boiler rooms that conduct lottery, sweepstakes, and other prize-related schemes targeting victims overseas.

➢ ***Caribbean***: Law enforcement intelligence and reporting by Jamaican news outlets document the rising popularity of lottery fraud schemes targeting U.S. residents among Kingston- and Montego Bay-based criminal enterprises. These operations are using police corruption, murder, kidnappings, robberies, and other violent tactics to discourage rival groups, compete for proceeds and lists of potential victims, and expand their operations.[28]

➢ ***Europe***: Intelligence from a number of law enforcement agencies indicates that mass-marketing fraud operations weave their way through multiple European countries. A United Kingdom law enforcement investigation found that a Spain-based boiler room operated largely by British expatriates, which solicits victims to purchase worthless or low-value US securities, has defrauded more than 15,000 citizens of the United Kingdom and other countries of more than £35 million. In addition, since 2003 the Spanish National Police, working with U.S. authorities, have arrested more than 400 individuals and identified more than 400 bank accounts used to perpetrate a fraudulent lottery targeting victims in Australia, Canada, the United Kingdom, the United States, and dozens of other countries.

Recent intelligence reveals that similar lottery fraud groups in Germany, the Netherlands, and the United Kingdom continue to contact victims, suggesting that the Spanish arrests only temporarily disrupted the fraud networks' operations. France, Germany, the Netherlands, Spain, and the United Kingdom also have been identified as hub countries for the flow of counterfeit checks and fraudulent mailings; indeed, authorities estimate that approximately 40,000 fraudulent letters leave Spain each day en route to victims around the world. Finally, Eastern Europe, and Romania in particular, has emerged as an epicenter of Internet-based mass-marketing fraud and other cyber crimes, spurred in part by stagnant economies and endemic public corruption that provide limited opportunities for legitimate employment and enable organized crime to flourish.

➢ ***Middle East***. Within the last two years, the Israel National Police, working with US law enforcement, have arrested more than 20 Israeli citizens and residents for perpetrating lottery fraud schemes that allegedly defrauded elderly US residents of $27 million.[29]

➢ ***North America***: In Canada and the United States, boiler rooms and smaller, less-formal mass-marketing fraud operations solicit Canadian, US, and foreign victims with fraudulent offers for medical treatments and cures, illegitimate business opportunities, high-risk investments, guaranteed credit cards and grants, low-interest loans, and over-priced office directories and supplies. Recent investigations have revealed that US-based fraudsters also target immigrants with false offers to assist applicants with obtaining legal immigration status, employment, and housing in the United States.

While some schemes are homegrown operations, locations outside North America are also popular with foreign fraudsters, who may exploit the host nations' abundance of cheap labor, existing call centers, and new communication technologies, such as Voice over Internet Protocol (VoIP), to disguise the locations from which they are calling. Indeed, Canadian intelligence suggests that aggressive law enforcement actions over the last decade have spurred many traditional boiler rooms to relocate to other regions. Certain Canadian and U.S. residents are known to have relocated operations to Costa Rica and Caribbean locations.

- *Foreign Outsourcing of Operations*. Law enforcement intelligence shows that fraudulent mass-marketing operations routinely outsource vital business functions, such as the printing of lottery mailings, the fulfillment of orders, and the laundering of fraud proceeds, to legitimate businesses and criminal enterprises around the world. United Kingdom authorities have identified fraudsters' use of companies in India, France, Germany, Hungary, and Morocco to print and bulk ship documents into the United Kingdom. Canadian boiler rooms frequently employ U.S.-based payment processors, brokers of "lead lists" (lists containing identifying data on prior fraud victims), and fulfillment centers to obtain access to the US banking system, target specific types of victims, and distribute worthless items that the fraudsters have fraudulently sold to consumers. Recent law enforcement investigations have also revealed that West African fraud groups routinely contract with Middle Eastern and Asian criminal enterprises to launder the proceeds of fraud schemes through the accounts of criminal conspirators, shell companies, and legitimate businesses and individuals that temporarily rent their accounts to perpetrators.

  > *Fraudulent mass-marketing operations routinely outsource vital business functions to legitimate businesses and criminal enterprises around the world.*

- *Involvement of Organized Criminal Enterprises*. Although mass-marketing fraud, as described elsewhere, can be conducted by a single individual or small groups of individuals, law enforcement intelligence reveals that organized criminal enterprises increasingly conduct, facilitate, and profit from international mass-marketing fraud schemes. These groups range from traditional, highly-structured enterprises, such as Cosa Nostra families in North America, to loosely-knit ethnic-based groups, such as Nigerian and Jamaican organizations. Many of these groups

  > *Organized criminal enterprises increasingly conduct, facilitate, and profit from international mass-marketing fraud schemes.*

demonstrate international reach, operating from multiple countries and continents and relying upon shared ethnic, national, family, tribal, or other ties to engender trust and enable cooperation among members for whom no direct connections exist.

The nature and degree of organized crime groups' involvement in mass-marketing fraud vary substantially. Some groups exercise control over all aspects of a fraud operation and other groups outsource or provide specialized support services, including mailing counterfeit documents, collecting victims' payments, hosting fraudulent web sites, supplying leads lists, forging identity documents and financial instruments, and laundering illicit proceeds. Organized crime groups are attracted to mass-marketing fraud's comparatively low risk of detection, prosecution, and incarceration (compared to other criminal activities), and vast profit potential, which may enable the groups to fund other criminal ventures. Reliable law enforcement intelligence indicates that some mass-marketing perpetrators routinely engage in other white-collar crime ventures, including government benefit fraud, credit card fraud, identity theft, mortgage fraud, and the sale of counterfeit goods. Less substantiated intelligence suggests that some fraud groups are also involved in drugs and arms trafficking.

II. METHODS AND TECHNIQUES OF MASS-MARKETING FRAUD

Types and Structures of Fraud Operations

Mass-marketing fraud operations vary widely in size, structure, and complexity. Depending on the nature of the scheme, they may range from one- and two-person entrepreneurial efforts and loosely-knit online groups to sophisticated, hierarchical boiler rooms and ethnic-based criminal enterprises. Despite such diversity, law enforcement intelligence suggests that, as a whole, fraudulent mass-marketing operations are increasingly transnational, interconnected, and fluid, with groups shifting alliances according to the particular needs of a scheme.

> *As a whole, fraudulent mass-marketing operations are increasingly transnational, interconnected, and fluid.*

Mass-marketing fraud boiler rooms tend to be highly-structured and high-pressure business operations in which small armies of managers and employees, armed with telephones or computers, rapidly pitch deceptive or misleading offers for merchandise and services to consumers around the world. Law enforcement intelligence indicates that many fraudulent boiler rooms are lead by recidivist offenders who possess long-term and substantial knowledge and experience establishing and overseeing complex boiler room operations, developing and approving misleading sales pitches, and directing the movement of illicit proceeds among bank accounts. While many boiler rooms are self-contained independent operations, recent law enforcement investigations suggest that more boiler rooms are outsourcing certain business functions to specialists and coordinating with criminal groups in other countries to broaden the reach of their fraud operations and launder funds. In addition, boiler rooms are increasingly employing countermeasures, including relocating frequently and using sophisticated technologies, to conceal their communications and the locations from which they operate. To avoid drawing unwanted law enforcement scrutiny, mass-marketing boiler rooms seldom use violence and corruption of individuals or businesses, except in rare incidents to discipline group members or further short-term objectives.

Law enforcement intelligence reveals regional variations in the types of fraud schemes that boiler rooms conduct. Within the United States and Canada, traditional organized crime groups such as La Cosa Nostra, outlaw motorcycle gangs, and other fraudsters use boiler rooms to promote illicit lotteries and sweepstakes, high-risk investment schemes, advance-fee loan and credit card offers, deceptive business opportunities, and fraudulent sales of merchandise and services. Romanian criminal enterprises employ boiler room-like structures to perpetrate organized Internet fraud schemes targeting consumers and merchants around the world. In the United Kingdom, the boiler room structure is predominately associated with investment frauds involving the fraudulent sale of worthless corporate shares. Israeli boiler rooms have been linked to lottery fraud schemes targeting elderly victims.

In contrast to boiler rooms, West African criminal enterprises engaged in mass-marketing fraud tend to be fluid, insular operations with few clear lines of communication or authority. These criminal organizations may form along tribal or family-relationship lines and appear to be of varying sizes, ranging from entrepreneurial efforts conducted by a few individuals with a computer and a cellular telephone to highly-organized operations involving many cells that coordinate as necessary to perpetrate one or multiple schemes. Recent investigations indicate that multiple cells or individuals can rapidly form criminal syndicates, using recommendations from other fraudsters to identify persons or groups that can facilitate different aspects of a scam, such as forging checks, mailing documents, laundering illicit proceeds, and posing as telephone references to verify a scam's legitimacy.

Such fraud syndicates are attenuated operations, in which conspirators routinely communicate via email, have little knowledge of the other participants' true identities, and cease contact at the conclusion of the scam. These loosely-connected cells are located around the world, including in Europe, Asia, the Middle East, North America, and South America; indeed, Canadian authorities estimate that more than 100 West African fraud groups are currently operating in British Columbia alone. Moreover, a single fraud scheme's operations can span multiple countries. Law enforcement intelligence suggests that the international dimension of these traditionally non-indigenous groups is evolving, as group members - who are drawn almost exclusively from members of the Nigerian or West African diaspora - seek permanent residency or citizenship in the countries to which they migrate. Whereas West African fraud groups historically routed illicit proceeds to and accepted direction from leaders within their countries of origin, recent intelligence suggests that members of such groups are increasingly assimilating into their new environments, retaining proceeds for personal use, and directing their own fraudulent operations.

West African criminal enterprises are highly adaptive and opportunistic, perpetrating nearly every type of mass-marketing fraud, including the ubiquitous 419 schemes as well as lottery, loan, investment, and work-at-home schemes. The groups often share successful fraud techniques with and provide assistance to other cells, a practice that may result in the commission of nearly-identical schemes by multiple groups acting in relative independence of one another. They frequently employ individuals with specialized skills to impersonate attorneys, government officials, and bankers; design web sites; forge checks; translate documents into foreign languages; collect wire transfers; and process incoming and outgoing mail. Many countries, including Canada, the Netherlands, the United Kingdom, and the United States, have noted the involvement of West African criminal networks in drugs and arms smuggling, human trafficking, and the organized export of stolen automobiles. However, the extent to which these criminal networks also engage in fraud is not well known, with some intelligence suggesting that fraud proceeds fund other criminal activities and other data indicating that fraud groups operate independently from other criminal groups.

The formal, efficiently-structured boiler room and the fluid, loosely-connected West African criminal network, while well-known to law enforcement investigators, represent just two of the many types of groups that perpetrate mass-marketing fraud. For example,

United States intelligence has identified the existence of less-structured boiler rooms, sometimes called "rip-and-tear rooms," which may arise when traditional boiler rooms close or when experienced telemarketers decide to become independent operators. Rip-and-tear rooms tend to be highly mobile, operating out of vehicles and hotel rooms, communicating with victims via cellular telephone and wireless Internet services, and collecting victims' funds from wire transfer outlets. Canadian and United States law enforcement investigations have also identified virtual criminal enterprises that consist of individuals around the world who only communicate via online forums yet engage in organized fraud schemes and identity theft.

Methods of Contacting Victims

Fraudulent mass-marketers reach victims via all modes of communication – postal service, telephone, e-mail, Internet sites, television, radio, and in some cases even in person. Victim reporting reveals that Internet-based solicitations are among the most common: in the United States, web sites and e-mails accounted for 60 percent of reported contacts in 2009, and Canada noted a 46 percent spike in Internet-related complaints from 2008 to 2009.[30] Nearly 70 percent of Australian victims reported fraudulent contact via the Internet.[31] In addition to serving as a primary method of contact, the Internet is also an effective tool for identifying potential victims. Law enforcement intelligence reveals perpetrators' increasing use of email spiders, which crawl through web sites, message boards, and other online forums to harvest email addresses for subsequent solicitation via spam email. Once the email addresses have been collected, fraudsters often employ botnets - networks of computers infected with malicious code and programmed to follow the directions of a common command-and-control server – to facilitate the simultaneous distribution of thousands of spam emails. Perpetrators also pose as buyers and sellers on online auction web sites, upload fake jobs to employment web sites, and create bogus user accounts on social networking and dating web sites to target new victims and initiate fraud schemes under the guise of legitimacy. While the majority of recipients deletes or ignores Internet-based solicitations, their widespread distribution ensures that some recipients will believe the messages to be credible and respond accordingly. In addition, some recipients may perceive the email solicitations to be fraudulent but respond anyway, thereby validating their email addresses to the fraudsters and increasing the likelihood of future fraudulent solicitations.

Telephone-initiated solicitations remain among the most widely-reported and profitable methods by which fraudsters contact victims. For example, 30 percent of Canadian complainants in 2009 reported that perpetrators contacted them via the telephone.[32] Law enforcement intelligence reveals fraudsters' use of sophisticated telephone technology, including VoIP and platform numbers, to create the appearance that they are operating within specific cities and countries. While nearly all fraud groups use the telephone to contact victims, boiler rooms specialize in the process of outbound telemarketing, purchasing lead lists and then cold-calling potential victims to induce the purchase of goods or services or to solicit a charitable contribution. Boiler rooms also engage in inbound telemarketing through the dissemination of advertisements and promotional materials, often promising awards and prizes for participation. These promised (but nonexistent) awards and prizes are designed to entice victims to contact the boiler rooms. Once prospective victims call in, telemarketers subject them to fraudulent or deceptive sales pitches. In contrast to outbound telemarketing rooms, which typically experience high rates of rejection when they initially contact prospective victims, inbound telemarketing efforts tend to produce the opposite effect. Those individuals who initiate contact with the boiler rooms, although a fraction of those who received the promotional materials, are often more inclined to accede to the telemarketers' sales pitches.

Critical Resources for Mass-Marketing Fraud Operations

Viable mass-marketing fraud groups require a variety of resources to operate, including the means to target and communicate with prospective victims, obtain and launder illicit proceeds, and evade law enforcement detection and investigation. These include the following:

- **Legitimate Business Services**. Operators of mass-marketing fraud schemes increasingly employ certain services of legitimate and semi-legitimate businesses, which may or may not be aware of the underlying fraud, to perform critical functions. Law enforcement intelligence reveals fraudsters' use of mailing houses to print, package, and ship counterfeit documents. To conceal the locations from which they operate, fraudsters may contract with virtual office companies, which provide accommodation addresses, collect mail, and forward telephone calls. Many fraud groups, especially boiler rooms that use deceptive and misleading pitches to sell products, employ customer service and fulfillment centers to receive customer complaints, discourage refund requests, and package and ship worthless or low-quality merchandise.

- **Lead Lists**. Fraud perpetrators purchase customized "lead lists" –sometimes known as "sucker lists" by fraudsters – that contain individuals' names and contact information compiled according to myriad demographic criteria, from direct marketing companies and leads lists brokers, some of which perform minimal or no verification of the legitimacy of the groups or persons who order the lists. In addition to sorting leads by age, income, and occupation, some list brokers also identify individuals, such as sweepstakes participants, who may be unusually vulnerable to deceptive solicitations. Lead lists are also available for purchase via online black markets, including full data leads containing individuals' financial account numbers and lists of chronic fraud victims, who repeatedly participate in new fraud schemes despite the protective efforts of friends, family, and law enforcement.

- **Payment Processors.** Illicit boiler rooms often engage the services of payment processors, typically processors that are well aware of the true nature of the boiler rooms' operations, to facilitate the collection of victim funds via non-cash processes, such as bank debits, remotely-created checks, and credit card charges.

- **Communications Tools.** All mass-marketing fraud groups, regardless of their level of sophistication, require access to communication tools and networks. Law enforcement investigations have revealed perpetrators' use of calling cards, cellular phones, and pre-paid SIM cards, the disposable nature of which hinders law enforcement efforts to determine users' identities. West African fraud groups employ free web-based email accounts, frequent multiple Internet cafes, and use Internet phones and other devices that supply instantaneous Internet connections to undermine investigative efforts to trace Internet Protocol addresses. Large scale boiler rooms are investing in sophisticated computer systems and storing servers in other countries, trusting that the complexity of cross-border cases deters law enforcement investigation. Recent investigations indicate that fraudsters manipulate the caller identification features of Internet-based technology, including VoIP and platform numbers, to create the appearance of operating within victims' cities or countries rather than from overseas locations

- **Fraudulent Identification Documents.** Fraudulent identification documents are among the most essential tools in a fraudster's arsenal. Counterfeit passports, driver's licenses, and work permits enable perpetrators to open bank accounts under assumed names, collect packages from courier services, obtain telephone service to contact victims, and rent properties to house fraud operations. Fraudsters routinely use multiple generic "pitch names" (names of nonexistent people) to communicate with and collect illicit proceeds from different victims, a technique that requires the possession of fraudulent identification documents to support each fake persona. Law enforcement intelligence has revealed that a single perpetrator may use hundreds of fraudulent identities and multiple perpetrators may use one common identity, undermining law enforcement efforts to locate perpetrators and intercept fraudulent wire transfers.

- **Counterfeit Financial Instruments.**
Mass-marketing fraud criminals continue to use counterfeit financial instruments, including checks and money orders, to facilitate many mass-marketing schemes, including overpayment, lottery, and employment fraud. Illicit mass-marketers use sophisticated software, commercial laser printers and scanners, and blank check stock to produce the fake checks and money orders. The counterfeit documents lack security features, but many closely resemble legitimate financial instruments and are of sufficient quality to deceive unwitting consumers and bank personnel. Although customs, postal, and law enforcement agencies have identified packages of counterfeit checks addressed to victims around the world, the fraudulent instruments appear to have the greatest impact on Canadian and US victims, who routinely use checks for personal and business purposes. In contrast, European

> *Mass-marketing fraud criminals continue to use counterfeit financial instruments, including checks and money orders, to facilitate many mass-marketing schemes.*

consumers and businesses rarely use checks for any purpose and may view the unsolicited delivery of such instruments with greater skepticism.

With respect to U.S. consumers in particular, fraudsters' use of counterfeit checks exploits a general lack of knowledge about United States banking laws, which allow rapid access to funds from most check deposits, often before a bank has confirmed the legitimacy of the checks. Many account holders interpret this availability of funds as an indication that a check is legitimate, and they follow perpetrators' instructions to withdraw and wire transfer all or a portion of the money overseas for payment of taxes, fees, and other expenses. Law enforcement intelligence indicates that fraud perpetrators routinely send counterfeit financial instruments through myriad countries and alternate their routes and shipment methods to circumvent law enforcement and customs investigations. Recent investigations by Nigerian authorities have resulted in the arrest of check-carrying couriers preparing to board flights to South Africa, the United Arab Emirates, the United Kingdom, and the United States, and in the seizure of bulk packages of checks destined for reshippers in France, Italy, and Spain.

Stack of Counterfeit Postal Service Money Orders Seized by U.S. Immigration and Customs, 2009 [Source: ICE]

Methods of Evading Law Enforcement

Operators of mass-marketing fraud schemes are highly adaptive, rapidly changing their methods and techniques to reduce the risks of law enforcement detection and investigation and to respond to consumer and business awareness of their current methods. Perpetrators routinely employ generic "pitch names," assume the identities of legitimate organizations and high-profile individuals, create fraudulent email accounts to support fake identities, and use fraudulent identification documents. Many fraud groups promote multiple deceptive and illicit offers, often at the same time, and may easily switch to new promotions should older promotions start to generate significant complaints or unwelcome attention.

Fraudsters often widely share effective fraud schemes and recycle pitch names with other groups, complicating law enforcement efforts to identify the perpetrators responsible for specific schemes and victims. Fraud schemes typically emphasize the need for urgency and secrecy in all transactions, restrictions that prevent victims from verifying a solicitation's legitimacy and isolate them from the protective efforts of family and friends. Mass-marketing fraud groups tend to operate as fully independent or semi-autonomous ventures, cooperating and sharing information on an ad-hoc and need-to-know basis, so that law enforcement disruption of one room or cell does not destroy the entire fraudulent operation. Furthermore, the owners, coordinators, and leaders may be the most difficult to identify and prosecute, as they may not be closely involved in the day-to-day operations of the boiler rooms or groups.

Mass-marketing perpetrators often route their communications, operations, and illicit proceeds through multiple states and countries to complicate investigations and hinder timely information sharing. Fraud groups typically use communication methods that are difficult to trace, including "disposable" cellular phones, subscriber identity module (SIM) cards, and VoIP services. Intelligence reveals perpetrators' increasing use of Internet phones and other devices that enable perpetrators to access the Internet via cellular networks, undermining law enforcement efforts to identify perpetrators' locations. Fraudulent proceeds often flow through cash-based systems, such as Western Union and MoneyGram, and bank accounts in countries with strict bank secrecy laws, rendering law enforcement efforts to trace the funds a difficult, if not impossible, task. Although a single fraudulent mass-marketing operation may acquire millions of dollars from its victims, perpetrators deliberately target victims in diverse locations, knowing that the losses to victims in any one jurisdiction may be deemed insufficient to warrant law enforcement investigation. Many groups outsource key functions, such as mail distribution, mail processing, money retrieval, and money laundering, to criminal facilitators in multiple countries to minimize law enforcement efforts to disrupt the fraudulent operations. Perpetrators also establish operations in foreign countries in which the challenges to investigation and prosecution are likely to be great, due to political, social, economic, and even language barriers. The organizations frequently operate with substantially-greater flexibility than law enforcement and may simply close and reopen elsewhere once authorities have surmounted such barriers to investigation.

Identity Theft and Money Laundering

Identity theft and money laundering continue to be critical components of various mass-marketing fraud schemes. When criminals purchase lead lists, including "full data" leads containing consumers' sensitive personal and financial information, from lead lists brokers and other fraud groups, and use those names without the authorization of those consumer, they are engaging in identity theft or identity fraud. Law enforcement intelligence has revealed mass-marketers' purchase of data from illicit online carding sites that trade in consumer data stolen via database breaches, phishing schemes, and other illegal methods. Mass-marketing perpetrators also commit identity theft to further scam operations, by counterfeiting and printing legitimate company or government checks to defraud consumers, illegally accessing business accounts at private courier services to purchase postage and mail documents, and creating counterfeit identification to collect victims' funds. Once in possession of victims' funds, fraudulent mass-marketers exploit informal and formal financial systems, including money service businesses, domestic and international banks, shell company accounts, and underground money transfer systems, to conceal the destinations and beneficiaries of the illicit proceeds.

Like all successful criminal enterprises, mass-marketing fraudsters take great care to conceal the origins, beneficiaries, destinations, and uses of their proceeds and to impede authorities' efforts to track and seize the funds. Recent mass-marketing fraud investigations reveal that fraudsters continue to request victim payments via cash-based methods, including checks, money orders, paper currency hidden within magazines and cards, and commercial wire transfer services, as well as bank debits, bank transfers, and credit card charges.

Fraudulent mass-marketers vary their choice of payment method according to the demands of particular schemes and the perceived advantages or vulnerabilities associated with each method. They seek payment methods that produce and maintain the fewest records, allow for the rapid attainment of funds, and enhance a scheme's legitimacy, thereby encouraging victim participation. Law enforcement has noted, for example, that boiler rooms engaged in investment fraud predominantly use bank transfers to collect victims' funds, likely because bank transfers enable the processing of high payment amounts and appear credible in the eyes of educated and affluent victims whom these schemes often target. In contrast, West African fraud groups commonly request payment via wire transfers, which produce minimal documentation, can often be collected with forged identification, and may be rapidly retrieved from nearly any location.

Law enforcement intelligence suggests that once victims have remitted payment, the illicit funds often begin a complex voyage through multiple countries before reaching their final destinations. Despite extensive law enforcement efforts to track victim funds, perpetrators' use of complex payment methods and multiple jurisdictions complicates efforts to identify the ultimate beneficiaries and uses of fraudulent funds. Law enforcement intelligence suggests that perpetrators use much of the money for personal enrichment, purchasing property, securities, and automobiles, or to open new businesses such as Internet cafes to facilitate fraud schemes. Despite anecdotal evidence that suggests some perpetrators use fraud proceeds to finance other criminal ventures such as narcotics and weapons trafficking, law enforcement investigations have produced little reliable information to support these allegations to date.

Fraudulent mass-marketers often engage the services of legitimate businesses, other criminal enterprises, and criminal facilitators to launder illicit proceeds. Canadian and U.S. authorities have recently disrupted an extensive network of corrupt and collusive MoneyGram and Western Union agents who fraudulently obtained operating licenses for the sole purpose of rapidly receiving and laundering victims' funds; new intelligence suggests that perpetrators are adapting to these law enforcement actions by diverting victim payments to corrupt wire transfer counters in the United Kingdom and elsewhere. Other fraud groups, including West Africans and Romanians, employ low-level criminals and immigrants armed with counterfeit identification to collect fraudulent payments from legitimate money transfer agents and financial institutions.

Law enforcement intelligence also reveals perpetrators' use of shell company accounts, some of which are operated by criminal enterprises that specialize in money laundering, located at financial institutions in Asia, the Caribbean, and the Middle East. Intelligence suggests that many of these accounts are long-established money laundering accounts, which are used to receive and process wire transfers for many different fraud groups and schemes. West African fraud groups have also developed networks of complicit account holders, who typically retain a percentage of the profits in exchange for allowing perpetrators to access and use their bank accounts to collect victim funds. Law enforcement investigations have revealed trade-based money laundering via legitimate and semi-legitimate merchants, including automobile dealers, cellular telephone suppliers, and electronics stores, which accept victims' funds as payment for products to be exported to Nigeria and other countries. While many of the merchants are ignorant of the fraudulent sources of such payments, some fraudsters operate retail businesses to serve as fronts for the laundering of illicit fraud proceeds. Nigerian authorities have also noted West African fraud groups' use of the hawala informal banking system to move funds from the Netherlands, Spain, and the United Kingdom to beneficiaries in Nigeria.

One disturbing trend is the increasing exploitation of fraud victims to receive and launder victim funds, or to receive and disburse counterfeit financial instruments. A typical mass-marketing fraud scheme, for example, may recruit individuals to work in such varied capacities as collecting wire transfers, depositing checks or shipping counterfeit checks to other victims, accepting deliveries of merchandise purchased with stolen credit cards, forwarding funds and products overseas, and serving as business account agents for foreign companies. In addition, recent investigations have uncovered a number of victims, who lost thousands or tens of thousands of dollars to one or more fraud schemes, and who then appear to knowingly participate in mass-marketing fraud schemes. Even after warnings from law enforcement or attempted interventions by family members, these victims risk criminal charges to collect fraudulent wire transfers from or ship counterfeit checks to other victims.

> *One disturbing trend is the increasing exploitation of fraud victims to receive and launder victim funds, or to receive and disburse counterfeit financial instruments.*

Use of Threats and Violence

While most mass-marketing fraud schemes are nonviolent in nature, law enforcement intelligence reveals that some fraud groups employ threats and coercive tactics against uncooperative victims, rival groups, and their own group members. Victims have reported that persons posing as law enforcement or government officials have threatened arrest, imprisonment, or the seizure of bank accounts and assets should they fail to comply with fraudsters' demands. Within the United States, victims of an online extortion scheme have received e-mails containing pictures of dead bodies and threatening bodily harm.[33] However, actual incidents of physical harm to victims are exceedingly rare, with very few exceptions in which victims traveled to meet with or search for mass-marketing criminals. In many such cases, insufficient evidence exists to establish whether the violent crimes were linked to the fraud schemes or whether the victims were simply in the wrong places at the wrong times.

Some fraud groups employ threats and coercive tactics against uncooperative victims, rival groups, and their own group members.

Recent law enforcement intelligence suggests that use of mass-marketing related intra- and inter-group violence is on the rise in some places. Open-source and law enforcement reporting indicate that competing gangs in Jamaica are using murder and other violent tactics to steal victim leads lists and lottery fraud proceeds.[34] In the United States, the operators of a New York-based stock boiler room affiliated with two Italian organized crime families admitted to controlling and disciplining employees with threats and actual violence, including beatings, stabbings, and kidnappings.[35] Nigerian authorities report that, while violent intra-group conflict may arise over the sharing of fraud proceeds, such acts are seldom reported to law enforcement, hindering efforts to gauge the extent of the violence.

Use of mass-marketing related intra- and inter-group violence is on the rise in some places.

CONCLUSION

International mass-marketing fraud, in all of its constantly evolving forms, poses a serious threat to individuals, businesses, and financial institutions around the world. Fraud perpetrators exploit global financial systems, communications networks, and markets to defraud victims, launder illicit proceeds, conceal the locations from which they operate, and engage legitimate businesses as unwitting conspirators in their criminal activities. Organized crime groups increasingly initiate, facilitate, and profit from mass-marketing fraud, using persuasion and manipulation to steal substantial amounts of money, estimated in the tens of billions of dollars worldwide, from vulnerable consumers. Mass-marketing fraud groups are highly adaptive, altering schemes and techniques to evade law enforcement scrutiny and respond to consumer awareness of fraud schemes.

To counter this threat effectively, investigative, law enforcement, and regulatory authorities in multiple countries – whether those countries are used as bases of operations for mass-marketing fraud schemes, targets of such schemes, or both -- will need to pursue five approaches in close coordination:

1. Expansion of their capability to gather and share intelligence on all aspects of mass-marketing fraud schemes and their key participants, including ringleaders and individuals who provide key services, such as money laundering, that facilitate or expand the schemes' operations. The sources of such intelligence should come from public complaint data, information required to be reported to and voluntarily shared with law enforcement and regulatory authorities, information developed through criminal and civil investigations in various jurisdictions, and survey and other statistical data.

2. Development and expansion of capacities for disruption of the operations of mass-marketing fraud schemes through lawful means. This should include the seizure of counterfeit financial instruments and documents used in such schemes, the use of "lead lists" (i.e., lists of information on persons who have been victimized in previous fraud schemes) obtained by law enforcement to identify and contact victims, and the seizure and forfeiture of the criminal proceeds of such schemes.

3. Expansion of public awareness and education programs to help individuals and businesses more readily recognize solicitations by mass-marketing fraud schemes and take action to avoid or minimize losses to such schemes.

4. Development of effective measures and structures to more promptly identify and support victims of mass-marketing fraud schemes (including intervention services or victim-support networks when appropriate) through public- and private-sector resources. This should include enhanced efforts to identify mass-marketing fraud victims who have suffered financially devastating losses,

particularly senior citizens or others who have little or no ability to recoup their losses through future employment.

5. Development and expansion of coordinated efforts among investigative, law enforcement, and regulatory agencies to use their enforcement powers against major mass-marketing fraud schemes. This should include cooperation among authorities at national and transnational levels to prioritize the use of enforcement resources against key individuals and operations, to establish investigative structures (e.g. joint task forces) best suited to conduct investigations of those individuals and operations, to expedite cooperation in specific investigations and prosecutions, and to draw on all available lawful measures for gathering evidence relevant to those prosecutions.

Each of these approaches has been adopted and used, though in widely varying degrees, by various countries. In combination, and if applied in a consistent manner, these approaches provide a firm basis for a fully coordinated multinational response to combating mass-marketing fraud.

Appendix

Principal Types of Mass-Marketing Fraud

Mass-marketing fraud encompasses a broad range of fraudulent and deceptive schemes designed to separate people and businesses from their property, money, services, or information. Many perpetrators use generic, well-known fraud templates, simply recycling and updating schemes that have proven successful in the past, although individual schemes may vary in nature, execution, and targeted victim population. The most effective and lucrative scheme variations are often widely replicated, as criminals aim to capitalize on victims' delayed recognition of fraudulent solicitations. Versions of the following schemes are among the most-frequently reported to law enforcement and consumer protection agencies in Africa, Australia, Europe, and North America.

- *Acquisition and Advertisement Fraud Targeting Businesses*: Businesses remain popular targets for fraud schemes, as employees may be less vigilant or capable of detecting and protecting against threats to corporate funds, and the amounts of money involved in fraudulent business transactions may be larger than schemes involving individuals. Many perpetrators use the "assumed sale" technique, misleading businesses to believe that someone within the company authorized a purchase, demanding payment for fictitious debts, and using fraudulent invoices and payment slips as proof of service. Perpetrators may also pose as legitimate venders or companies' usual suppliers to solicit the sale of expensive or low-quality office products, advertisements in nonexistent or poorly-distributed business directories, and poorly-crafted web sites. Belgian and Dutch authorities have identified schemes involving the fraudulent sale of domain names, web addresses, and domain extensions at inflated prices.

- *Charity Schemes:* Perpetrators of charity fraud schemes exploit sympathetic causes, legitimate charities, holiday seasons, and humanitarian, environmental, and other disasters to solicit financial contributions. Instead of using donated funds for their stated charity or cause, however, perpetrators retain and use all or most of the money for personal enrichment and other improper purposes.

- *Counterfeit Check Fraud Schemes (Including Schemes Targeting Attorneys):* A variety of mass-marketing fraud schemes, including lottery schemes and online auction schemes, commonly use counterfeit checks or counterfeit money orders to enhance the perceived legitimacy of a transaction. Whether sent to a victims as a disbursement of lottery winnings or payment for a high-value item such as a car, the fraudsters always require that the recipient deposit the check or money order into his or her bank account, then transfer a portion of the face amount of the check or money order back to them. Several weeks later, the bank into which the check or money order was deposited informs the depositor that the financial instrument was counterfeit and holds the depositor liable for the full face value of the instrument.

Law enforcement has identified an emerging scheme in which perpetrators are targeting attorneys and law firms. Posing as representatives of foreign companies, the perpetrators request legal assistance to collect delinquent payments from vendors or customers. At the behest of the foreign companies, the targeted law firms pursue payment from the alleged debtors, receive checks payable to the law firms, and forward the balance of the payment, less the firms' fees, to the perpetrators. More recent variations of the scheme involve perpetrators posing as individuals seeking resolution of personal injury claims and wives requesting legal assistance to collect divorce settlements from their ex-husbands.

- *Emergency Assistance Schemes*: Perpetrators, posing as a family member or close friend, contact victims with requests for urgent financial assistance, claiming that a family member was arrested overseas and requires bail money or a friend had an accident and needs funds for emergency medical expenses.

- *Foreign Lottery and Sweepstakes Fraud:* Perpetrators of lottery, sweepstakes, and prize schemes target unwitting individuals with false promises of money or valuable items, provided that the victims first purchase certain products or make advance payments of fictitious fees and taxes. Perpetrators often use counterfeit financial instruments to enhance these schemes' appearance of credibility.

- *Investment Fraud:* Perpetrators of investment fraud schemes, including penny stock schemes, advance-fee recovery schemes, and high-yield investment programs (also known as "Ponzi" schemes), target victims with fraudulent promises of high returns in exchange for devoting investment funds to the purchase of securities, real estate, stakes in oil drilling ventures, coins, gems, and other commodities.

- *Merchandise Purchase / Product Misrepresentation Schemes:* Merchandise purchase fraud comprises a wide range of schemes that target consumers who purchase or attempt to purchase products or services via Internet auction sites, catalogs, mail order services, classified advertisements, and other media. Common schemes include perpetrators' failure to deliver purchased merchandise, delivery of purchased goods later than promised, delivery of worthless or significantly less-valuable items than purchased, and misrepresentation of products' true conditions. While perpetrators can offer any item for sale, analysis of Canadian fraud complaints suggests that popular and trendy technologies such as iPhones, laptops, digital cameras, and video game consoles are among the most commonly advertised. Nigerian and US authorities have identified similar schemes involving the fraudulent sale of pets, magazines, office supplies, vacations and timeshares, health products, precious stones, and scrap metals. Some perpetrators send consumers and businesses bills for unordered products, demanding payment and threatening legal action to collect the fraudulent debt In another common scheme, perpetrators target users of legitimate online auction sites by offering losing bidders a second chance to purchase the desired products, provided that the buyers pay via wire transfer or other unsecure payment method.

- *Psychic/Clairvoyant Schemes:* Perpetrators of psychic/clairvoyant schemes contact victims with offers to make predictions of events that will change victims' lives, provided that the victims pay in advance. Perpetrators may entice victims with predictions of extreme good fortune and threaten bad luck should victims fail to comply with the demands for money.

- *Recovery Schemes:* Perpetrators of recovery schemes, often posing as lawyers, law enforcement officials, or government employees, target prior scam victims with offers to facilitate restitution pursuant to the advance payment of administrative and other fees.

- *Romance Schemes*: Perpetrators of romance schemes target users of Internet dating and social networking sites by feigning romantic interest, securing victims' trust and affection through regular intimate conversations and exchanges of gifts, and then exploiting the relationship to fraudulently obtain money and valuable merchandise. Romance scam victims have reported sending money to facilitate the purchase of travel documents and airline tickets, pay for medication and hospital bills, fund charitable works programs, and help perpetrators recover from personal financial difficulties. While all mass-marketing schemes take a psychological toll on victims, romance schemes often leave victims emotionally devastated.

- *Sale of Merchandise / Overpayment Schemes:* In "sale of merchandise" or overpayment schemes, perpetrators remit fraudulent payments, often in the form of a counterfeit or altered monetary instruments, to purchase high-value products or services such as cars, computers, or electronic goods. The monetary instruments are generally payable in amounts greater than the products' advertised prices, and perpetrators instruct the sellers to deposit or cash the checks and return the balance by wire transfer. Belgian authorities have noted that criminal exploitation of certain online automobile sales sites is so prevalent that sellers now receive almost only fraudulent offers, many of which use fake escrow services to enhance the legitimacy of the bid. Perpetrators of other "sale of merchandise" schemes use stolen credit cards to purchase high-value retail items; in many cases, the businesses ship the products before discovering that the credit cards are stolen.

- *Service Schemes:* Similar to product misrepresentation schemes, service schemes involve false or misleading promotions for services. Canadian and U.S. victims have reported fraudulent offers for local and long-distance telecommunication services; Internet services; health and medical services; energy services; automobile sales, insurance, and warranties; dating services; immigration and green card application services; and financial services, including debt management, credit protection, and credit repair programs.

- *Traditional West African Fraud Schemes:* Traditional West African fraud schemes, often termed "419" frauds after the section of the Nigerian criminal code pertaining to fraud, entice victims with promises of immediate and enormous wealth. Common West African fraud solicitations include *inheritance schemes*, in which perpetrators require victims to pay fictitious fees and taxes to claim the nonexistent estates of previously-unknown and now-deceased relatives, and *black-money schemes* that solicit victims to purchase special cleansers to remove dye from paper currency that has, for various reasons, been blackened and rendered unusable. Perpetrators of *funds transfer schemes* claim to need a victim's financial assistance to transfer or embezzle money, often millions of dollars, from a foreign country or company in exchange for a portion of the stolen funds.

End Notes

[1] *See* U.S. Department of Justice Press Release (January 12, 2010) (sentencing of Ponzi scheme operator who used telephone, mail, investment seminars, and personal meetings with victims), *available at* http://losangeles.fbi.gov/dojpressrel/pressrel10/la011210.htm.

[2] In Canada, victims may report fraud to the Canadian Anti-Fraud Call Centre (managed by the Ontario Provincial Police, the Royal Canadian Mounted Police, and the Competition Bureau Canada) and Reporting Economic Crime Online (which uses the acronym RECOL and is administered by the National White Collar Crime Centre of Canada). In the United States, victims may report fraud to the Federal Trade Commission's Consumer Sentinel and the Internet Crime Complaint Center, a partnership between the National White Collar Crime Center, the Federal Bureau of Investigation, and the Bureau of Justice Assistance. In the United Kingdom, the National Fraud Reporting Centre is slated to become operational in 2010. In Belgium, citizens may contact eCops, an online reporting center administered by the Ministry of Economy and the Federal Computer Crimes Unit, to report online crimes, including spam emails, in which they have not been victimized. Belgium anticipates that eCops will accept official complaints beginning in 2010 or 2011; however, current fraud victims must still contact local law enforcement agencies to file official complaints.

[3] *See* Competition Bureau Canada, *2007 Canadian Consumer Mass Marketing Fraud Survey* (February 2008), *available at* http://www.ic.gc.ca/eic/site/ic1.nsf/vwapj/Environics-Competition%20Bureau-MMF-FinalRReport-Feb2008.pdf/$file/Environics-Competition%20Bureau-MMF-FinalRReport-Feb2008.pdf.

[4] Office of Fair Trading, *Research on impact of mass-marketed scams: A summary of research into the impact of scams on UNITED KINGDOM consumers* (December 2006), *available at* http://www.oft.gov.UnitedKingdom/shared_oft/reports/consumer_protection/oft883.pdf.

[5] *See id.*

[6] *See* Australian Bureau of Statistics, Personal Fraud, 2007 (June 27, 2008), *available at* http://www.abs.gov.au.

[7] *See* Federal Trade Commission, *Consumer Fraud in the United States: The Second FTC Survey* (October 2007), *available at* http://www.ftc.gov/opa/2007/10/fraud.pdf.

[8] With respect to Australia, Australian Bureau of Statistics data show that as of June 30, 2007, the estimated resident population 15 years and older was 16,939,731. Australian Bureau of Statistics, Australian Demographic Statistics, December Quarter 2007 (June 24, 2008), *available at* http://www.abs.gov.au. Using an estimated population of 230,173,211 U.S. adults, 5 percent of that population would be approximately 11,508,660. That latter total would be 14.279 times the size of the Australian population of 806,000 victims, and 25.4 times the 453,100 Australian victims who reported losses. Multiplying the total

Australian losses of AU $977 million (U.S. $905.7 million) by 25.4 equals US $23.004 billion. With respect to the United Kingdom, 6.5 percent of the 2008 U.S. population would be 14,961,259. That total would be 4.675 times greater than the U.K. victim population. Multiplying £3.5 billion by 4.675 would equal £16.36 billion, or US $24.65 billion.

[9] *See* Federal Trade Commission, Consumer Sentinel Network Data Book for January – December 2009 at 7 (February 2010), *available at* http://www.ftc.gov/sentinel/ reports/sentinel-annual-reports/sentinel-cy2009.pdf.

[10] *Id*. at 7 n.2. In contrast, 267 consumers in 2007 and 257 consumers in 2008, respectively, reported that they had lost $1 million or more to consumer fraud. *Id.*

[11] *See* Canadian Anti-Fraud Centre, *Annual Statistic Report 2009: Mass-Marketing Fraud and ID Theft Activities, available at* www.phonebusters.com/english/documents/ AnnualStatisticalReport2009_001.pdf.

[12] *See* Australian Competition and Consumer Commission, *Targeting Scams: Report of the ACCC on Scam Activity 2009* (March 1, 2010), *available at* http://www.accc.gov.au/content/item.phtml?itemId=916075&nodeId=3742e183615bf4c0b1 38d4d1a165232d&fn=Targeting%20scams%202009.pdf

[13] *See* Competition Bureau Canada, *2007 Canadian Consumer Mass Marketing Fraud Surv*ey (February 2008), *available at* http://www.ic.gc.ca/eic/site/ic1.nsf/vwapj/Environics- Competition%20Bureau-MMF-FinalRReport-Feb2008.pdf/$file/Environics- Competition%20Bureau-MMF-FinalRReport-Feb2008.pdf.

[14] *See Massive Taiwanese-led phone scam uncovered, 94 arrests*, Chiang Mai Mail, July 28 – August 3, 2009, *available at* http://www.chiangmai-mail.com/336/.

[15] *See* Curt Anderson, *AP: Ponzi collapses nearly quadrupled in '09*, Boston.com, December 28, 2009, *available at* http://www.boston.com/business/articles/2009/12/28/ ap_ponzi_collapses_more_than_tripled_in_09/

[16] *See* Associated Press, *50-Year Term for Minnesota Man in $3.7 Billion Ponzi Fraud*, New York Times, April 8, 2010, *available at* http://www.nytimes.com/2010/04/09/ business/09ponzi.html .

[17] *See, e.g.,* Warren Richey, *How Scott Rothstein rode $1.2 billion Ponzi scheme to wealth and power*, Christian Science Monitor, January 27, 2010, *available at* http://www.csmonitor.com/USA/2010/0127/How-Scott-Rothstein-rode-1.2-billion-Ponzi- scheme-to-wealth-and-power; U.S. Department of Justice, Press Release (April 15, 2009), *available at* http://www.justice.gov/opa/pr/2009/April/09-crm-352.html.

[18] *See* Nick O'Malley, *Warrant issued over $1.5b alleged fraud*, Sydney Morning Herald, November 5, 2009, *available at* http://www.smh.com.au/national/warrant-issued-over-15b-alleged-fraud-20091105-hybh.html.

[19] *See* AARP Foundation, *Off the Hook: Reducing Participation in Telemarketing Fraud* (2003), *available at* http://assets.aarp.org/rgcenter/consume/d17812_fraud.pdf. In general, fraud losses tend to vary by scam type. For example, the United Kingdom and other countries have noted that one-time schemes such as prize draws, sweepstakes, and Internet auction fraud generally result in smaller loss amounts. In contrast, lotteries, investment frauds, and dating schemes, which are recurrent and sophisticated schemes that require victims to place long-term trust in perpetrators, accrue significant losses spanning multiple payments. Many countries, including Belgium, Canada, and the United States, have reported that complaints and investigations of Internet fraud schemes have risen in recent years.

[20] *See* Wesley Johnson, *Briton suffers 'romance fraud' kidnap ordeal*, Independent, January 12, 2010, *available at* http://www.independent.co.uk/news/uk/crime/briton-suffers-romance-fraud-kidnap-ordeal-1865551.html; Dan Goodin, *Irish man rescued after falling for 419 scam*, The Register, November 1, 2007, *available at* http://www.theregister.co.uk/2007/11/01/419_victim_rescued/.

[21] *See Seven in court for 419 scam kidnapping*, South Africa Dispatch, October 1, 2008, *available at* http://www.dispatch.co.za/article.aspx?id=255017.

[22] *See* Office of Fair Trading, *Research on impact of mass-marketed scams: A summary of research into the impact of scams on United Kingdom consumers* (December 2006), *available at* http://www.oft.gov.UnitedKingdom/shared_oft/reports/consumer_protection/oft883.pdf.

[23] Certain mass-marketing fraudsters – most notably, Ponzi scheme operators – often conduct their schemes in the same jurisdictions as their intended victims, *See, e.g.,* Melissa Grace, *Set of identical twins busted in long-term $2M investment scam*, New York Daily News, December 30, 2009, *available at* http://www.nydailynews.com/money/2009/12/30/2009-12-30_twins_busted_in_2m_invest_scam.html; Justin McCurry, *Arrests made in what could be biggest investment scam in Japanese history*, Guardian, February 5, 2009, *available at* http://www.guardian.co.United Kingdom/business/2009/feb/05/japan-kazutsugi-nami-ladies-gentlemen.

[24] *See 9 Cameroonians arrested for fraud*, Shenzhen Daily, March 19, 2010, *available at* http://szdaily.sznews.com/html/2009-03/19/content_554261.htm. The growth of mass-marketing fraud groups in other African countries may be due, in part, to enhanced enforcement efforts within Nigeria in the last decade. During that period, Nigerian law enforcement and postal authorities collaborated with foreign police and customs agencies to

disrupt fraudulent mass-marketing operations, arrest their leaders, and seize illegally-obtained assets and funds.

[25] *See* Jon Fernquest, *Arrests in transnational fraud* case, Bangkok Post, November 9, 2009, *available at* http://www.readbangkokpost.com/easybusinessnews/arrests_in_transnational_fraud.php.

[26] *See, e.g.*, Linda Smith, *Scams cost us dearly*, Hobart Mercury, April 5, 2010, *available at* http://www.themercury.com.au/article/2010/04/05/137991_tasmania-news.html

[27] *See Gold Coast woman recovers money from Nigerian fraud*, ABC News, March 29, 2010, *available at* http://www.abc.net.au/news/stories/2010/03/29/2859393.htm.

[28] For more information, see "Jamaican Gangsters Killed over Lottery Scam," *The Jamaica Observer*, October 2006, *available at* www.crimes-of-persuasion.com/Crimes/Telemarketing/Outbound/Major/jamaican-lottery-scam.htm, Adrian Frater, "Montego Bay Scam Investigation in US," *The Jamaica Gleaner*, 25 November 2007, *available at* www.jamaica-gleaner.com/gleaner/20071125/news/news1.html, and Noel Thompson, "Lottery Scam Causing Many of Montego Bay's Murders," *The Jamaica Gleaner*, 9 March 2009, *available at* www.jamaica-gleaner.com/gleaner/20090309/news/news2.html.

[29] *See* U.S. Department of Justice, Press Release, *Eleven Arrested in Israel on US Charges for Phony "Lottery Prize" Scheme that Targeted Elderly Victims in US* (21 July 2009), *available at* http://newyork.fbi.gov/dojpressrel/pressrel09/nyfo072109.htm, and U.S. Department of Justice, Press Release, *Israel-Based Defendants Indicted and Arrested in Lottery Telemarketing Fraud Targeting US Citizens* (26 September 2008), *available at* http://newyork.fbi.gov/dojpressrel/pressrel08/lottery092608.htm.

[30] *See* U.S. Federal Trade Commission, *Consumer Sentinel Network Data Book for January –December 2009* (February 2010), *available at* www.ftc.gov/sentinel/reports/sentinel-annual-reports/sentinel-cy2009.pdf, and Canadian Anti-Fraud Centre, *Annual Statistic Report 2009: Mass-Marketing Fraud and ID Theft Activities*, *available at* www.phonebusters.com/english/documents/AnnualStatisticalReport2009_001.pdf.

[31] Australian Competition and Consumer Commission, *Targeting Scams: Report of the ACCC on Scam Activity 2009* (March 1, 2010), *available at* http://www.accc.gov.au/content/item.phtml?itemId=916075&nodeId=3742e183615bf4c0b138d4d1a165232d&fn=Targeting%20scams%202009.pdf.

[32] Canadian Anti-Fraud Centre, *Annual Statistic Report 2009: Mass-Marketing Fraud and ID Theft Activities*, *available at* www.phonebusters.com/english/documents/AnnualStatisticalReport2009_001.pdf.

[33] *See* Internet Crime Complaint Center, *Alert: E-mails Containing Threats and Extortion*, December 2006, *available at* www.ic3.gov/media/2006/061207.htm.

[34] For more information, see "Jamaican Gangsters Killed over Lottery Scam," *The Jamaica Observer*, October 2006, *available at* www.crimes-of-persuasion.com/Crimes/ Telemarketing/Outbound/Major/jamaican-lottery-scam.htm, Adrian Frater, "Montego Bay Scam Investigation in US," *The Jamaica Gleaner*, 25 November 2007, *available at* www.jamaica-gleaner.com/gleaner/20071125/news/news1.html, and Noel Thompson, "Lottery Scam Causing Many of Montego Bay's Murders," *The Jamaica Gleaner*, 9 March 2009, *available at* www.jamaica-gleaner.com/gleaner/20090309/news/news2.html.

[35] *See* U.S. Department of Justice, Press Release, *Seven Members and Associates of the Colombo and Luchese Organized Crime Families Plead Guilty to Racketeering and Extortion in Connection with Boiler Room Stock Fraud Schemes* (April 2007), *available at* www.usdoj.gov/usao/nye/pr/2007/2007Apr17.html.